YOUR KNOWLEDGE H

Manü Mohr

Nostalgic memories. Perspective and perspectival changes in text and film of "A Child's Christmas in Wales"

GRIN Verlag

Bibliografische Information der Deutschen Nationalbibliothek:

Die Deutsche Bibliothek verzeichnet diese Publikation in der Deutschen National-
bibliografie; detaillierte bibliografische Daten sind im Internet über http://dnb.d-
nb.de/ abrufbar.

Imprint:

Copyright © 2013 GRIN Verlag GmbH
Druck und Bindung: Books on Demand GmbH, Norderstedt Germany
ISBN: 978-3-656-54859-1

GRIN - Your knowledge has value

Der GRIN Verlag publiziert seit 1998 wissenschaftliche Arbeiten von Studenten, Hochschullehrern und anderen Akademikern als eBook und gedrucktes Buch. Die Verlagswebsite www.grin.com ist die ideale Plattform zur Veröffentlichung von Hausarbeiten, Abschlussarbeiten, wissenschaftlichen Aufsätzen, Dissertationen und Fachbüchern.

Visit us on the internet:

http://www.grin.com/

http://www.facebook.com/grincom

http://www.twitter.com/grin_com

1. Introduction

Christmas... that magic blanket that wraps itself about us,
that something so intangible that it is like a fragrance. It may weave a spell of nostalgia.
Christmas may be a day of feasting, or of prayer,
but always it will be a day of remembrance,
a day in which we think of everything we have ever loved.

This quote by Augusta E. Rundel illustrates so well the innermost feelings of the speaker in Dylan Thomas' *A Child's Christmas in Wales*, who reminisces about the most beautiful time of the year he passed with family and friends. However, he does not just recount facts in an emotionally detached way; and it is the aim of this term paper to analyze the confounding of the adult and the child speaker, that is, the former being entirely plunged in his memories surrounding him "like a fragrance", he seems to actually *be* the child he was, reliving some scenes again.

First of all, after having given some information about the text version of Thomas' work, I will introduce Gérard Genette's theory of narratology, and mainly focus on the distinction between narration and focalization. This subtle difference, as well as other terminology referring to the question of perspective, is very enriching, as it permits to localize the narrator's point of view and involvement, to understand the story's organization, and eventually, to reflect on the how and why of the blurring of boundaries between the adult speaker of the here and now (at the moment of speaking), and the child speaker experiencing the events. I will argue that those two are intertwined, with several gradations more or less explicit in text and film.

Next, the way of narrating, the style, and linguistic issues will be examined, in order to attribute certain expressions or sentence structures either rather to the adult, or to the child. Of course it is not always possible to draw a clear-cut line, but nevertheless, there are passages which I believe to be revealing when arguing in favor of a perspective. It is crucial not to forget that the latter does not stay static, but that we can detect shifts of position throughout the story. This gives reason to dwell on some scenes in further detail.

The second part of my work will deal with the film *A Child's Christmas in Wales*. As above, I will begin with some general remarks; then I would like to investigate the impact of the camera position because a stage director, by means of making different choices concerning distance, or angle of vision, can influence the spectators' perception, and thus, partially, their emotions.

Finally, the role of sounds and music will be taken into consideration, there will be a close analysis of a few scenes, and I will sum up my results in the conclusion.

2. *A Child's Christmas in Wales:* The Text

A Child's Christmas in Wales is a prose poem, published as a book for the first time in 1954, which has its origins in two distinct works. The first one, *Memories of Christmas*, has been suggested by the producer of The Welsh Children's Hour of the B.B.C. in 1945. For fear of a displeasing incident, "[t]hey had to pretend to Thomas, who is hardly likely to have cared anyway, that technical reasons made it necessary to record in advance" (Ferris 200-201). This part contains the passage with the fire in the Prothero's kitchen, and is particularly close to poetry. "Conversation About Christmas", the second work, is an essay written for *Picture Post* in 1947.

A Child's Christmas in Wales is among Dylan Thomas' most famous and successful works. It has been adapted as numerous theater plays, and film, on which I will focus later on. It is a very nostalgic portrait of Christmas Eve; the story is made up of several anecdotes rather than being a chronological report. The touching poeticity of language (see the chapter on style), and the beautiful depiction of childhood memories have often been considered as being in sharp contrast to Dylan Thomas the persona (cf Korg 16). 'A condemnable artist could not but produce meritless art' - this alludes to Thomas' writings with provocative or disturbing subjects for his time. But in the following, there will not be given voice to these discussions – I would like to look at the work independently of the author's life, and underline the elaborated way of representing an adult's rediscovery of a child's delight in Christmas.

3. Gérard Genette's theory

The terminology introduced by the French literary theorist Gérard Genette in his work *Narrative Discourse. An Essay in Method*, first published in 1972, will provide a basis for my analysis of perspective and perspectival changes in Dylan Thomas' work. I present and explain his definition of narration and focalization, as well as other important aspects which play a role in my analysis in terms of the point of view.

To begin with, there are two decisive points one has to keep in mind : firstly, Genette's classification system is very strict, but detailed, and allows an exact identification of many narrative phenomena we encounter not only in contemporary, but also in historical texts. The "context of production as a fundamental element" comes to the fore (Guillemette and Lévesque). Secondly, Genette is convinced that every narrative, regardless of how it seems at first sight, implies the presence of a narrator. There can be no story without a narrator presenting the events in a certain way, because could be possible that the narrator makes himself explicit at any time in the story.

As I said above, I will accentuate the distinction between narration and focalization, following closely Genette's definitions. The first, often referred to as 'voice', is defined as the question: who speaks? One component in particular must be mentioned, namely the narrative levels, which are also going to be relevant for my perspectival analysis. The diegesis is the story, with the extradiegetic level being the so-called 'level of transmission' where the main plot is located; whereas the second, intradiegetic level, is concerned with the events presented in the narrative. A third, metadiegetic level, is provided within the second one. The difference between them is "that any event a narrative recounts is at a diegetic level immediately higher than the level at which the narrating act producing this narrative is placed" (Genette 228). Furthermore, the author talks about the possibilities of the narrator's relation with the story. Of course, the question of the personal involvement is relevant for the comprehension of the narrator's position and the nostalgic undertone in *A Child's Christmas in Wales*.

Instead of working with the expressions of a first-person or third-person narrator (used for example by Franz K. Stanzel), Gérard Genette, having realized the need for a new typology, uses other concepts who answer the question of the narrator's relation to the story. A homodiegetic one is present in the narrated world and takes part in his own story. At the highest form of involvement, the narrator coincides with the protagonist, and is thus called autodiegetic. By contrast, the heterodiegetic narrator manifests the greatest distance, being almost, though never entirely, absent from the story.

Focalization, or the narrative mood, gives an answer to the question: who sees in the story? It is about the narrator's consciousness, and all he can perceive and feel. Various nuances are imaginable here; and the choice amongst them, or the combination of multiple ones, can have an impact on the addressee's understanding and feelings. An external focalization signifies that the narrator remains as neutral as possible, and that he has no insight in the characters thoughts. Often, this position is compared to a camera simply showing the actions. When the narrator knows more than a character, or even everything about all characters, this is a case of zero-focalization. The omniscient narrator's knowledge is not restricted. Finally, the internal focalization displays a narrator knowing as much as one character.

Obviously, there are much more ways an author can construct and organize a story by modifying other narrative devices, such as order, duration or frequency (see the first chapters in Genette). Nonetheless, already these basic assumptions Gérard Genette makes in his work are going to be really helpful when I now highlight the narrative situations in Dylan Thomas' prose poem.

4. The way of narrating

"You can struggle with rhyme and meter and style and still not have a poem", said Dylan Thomas once (qtd. in Baughan Murdy, 107). In my opinion, it is legitimate not only to claim that *A Child's Christmas in Wales* bears resemblance to a poem, but also that some aspects which hold for Thomas' poetry are true for the short story in question. But what are the main features all poems have in common?

According to Vera and Ansgar Nünning, the characteristics are relative brevity, density and reduction of the topic, subjectivity, musicality, and deviations from everyday language (47-49). By definition, short stories fulfill the first condition: they begin *in medias res* and can be read in one single sitting. With Thomas' short story, this is perfectly possible. The second requirement goes hand in hand with the first one, and again we could say the same thing is true for short stories, which nearly always concentrate on only one line of action and one subject-matter. Also the third point is suitable for a formal description of short stories. Naturally, many people like to think back at how they celebrated Christmas when they were children; however, in our short story by Dylan Thomas, the narrator gives an account of his personal Christmas Eve. Now I will discuss he last two criteria, concerning more precisely stylistic and linguistic issues.

Many authors have pointed out the need to read out aloud Dylan Thomas' works, including those not intended to be broadcast on the radio. The author himself was convinced that poetry was "the rhythmic [...] movement from an overclothed blindness to a naked vision" (qtd. by Stearns in Tedlock 119). Louise Baughan Murdy also emphasized the value of an oral reading, and links this to the possibility of a deeper understanding of the texts : "[...] Thomas himself felt that auditory effects contribute to the total meaning of a poem" (11). It is via the listening that we understand that sound and sense go together, and that the meaning rather lies in the former than in thought. In *A Child's Christmas in Wales*, we can detect a lot of affinities with poetry: from the very beginning of the text, the author uses alliterations and internal rhymes. When looking closely at the first paragraph, one sees that the [s]- and [z]-sounds prevail (I stick to the phonetic notation as given in the International Phonetic Alphabet). For example, we have "sound except the distant speaking of voices I sometimes hear" (my emphasis, also in the following). Furthermore, the diphthong [aʊ] appears frequently: "ar**ou**nd the sea-t**ow**n corner n**ow** and **out** of all s**ou**nd". Also the second paragraph of the short story contains alliterations, such as "**t**oward the **t**wo-**t**ongued sea", "**f**ish-**f**reezing waves", or "**w**ool-**w**hite". In order to confirm the rhythmicity Dylan Thomas himself has talked about, we can have a look at the passage in which the children play a game: "Now we were snow-blind travelers / lost on the north hills, / and vast dewlapped dogs, / with flasks round their necks / ambled and shambled up to us, / baying 'Excelsior'".

Elder Olson goes in for morphology, syntax, and semantics, writing that Thomas both liked to create new words with multiple meanings and functions in a phrase, and to use many metaphors (54-56). We find "Christmases roll down", "a dumb, numb thunder-storm of white, torn Christmas cards", or "ice-cream hills". An example for the attribution of a new meaning to a word could be "wind-cherried noses", that is 'to have a nose as red as a cherry due to the wind', because 'to cherry' does not exist with the required meaning.

I thus conclude that *A Child's Christmas in Wales* has indeed several properties in common with poetry. However, this raises the question of artificiality and authenticity. On the one hand, given that in Nünning "deviations from everyday language" (47) are likewise cited among the characteristics of a poem, this could be interpreted as creating a distance. Clearly, it cannot be a child who is speaking in such an elaborate way, although the author often aims at imitating a child's point of view, as we will see in the following analysis. On the other hand, Thomas also tried to render the nostalgic atmosphere and feelings. The poetic language, and the complex structure on all linguistic sub-fields, certainly contribute to the romantic style, the idyllic picture of Christmas Eve, as well as to the impression to share the same dear memories with the narrator. Dylan Thomas' story is personal and universal at the same time: the latter, because he captures the essence, so to speak, or the major elements of Christmas how anyone of us could perceive them; and personal, because his family served as an inspiration:

> His [Thomas' grandfather's] was a large family, and when he died in 1905, there were three sons and four daughters still alive. These, with their husbands and wives, are the uncles and aunts of Dylan's *A Child's Christmas in Wales*, sturdy, humble people. (Fitzgibbon 15)

What is more, neither does the short story's title allow for an identification of a single person, and the author has preferred the more general formulation to the possibility to say 'my Christmas in Wales'. Speaking in Gérard Genette's terms, when only considering the title, we could be confronted with a heterodiegetic, covert narrator who has knowledge either about all characters, only one, or none. I will show that some of these options can be excluded by further analysis.

The aspect of the narrator's reliability gives more insight into the latter's status and position. His (non-)trustworthiness, and the (non-)exactness of facts, affect the perception of the work. In *A Child's Christmas in Wales*, besides the fact that the narrator is personally involved (in fact, he is not only homo-, but autodiegetic), he hints at the possible incorrectness of his memories. The famous "[…] I can never remember whether it snowed for six days and six nights when I was twelve or whether it snowed for twelve days and twelve nights when I was six" is a passage where the narrator admits that he does not remember every detail any more. Also the metaphor "Christmases roll down" could be a sign of unreliability, meaning that the memories got mixed up. Some other examples, thanks to which we identify the autodiegetic narrator, are the rectification "we never heard Mrs. Prothero's first cry […]. Or, if we heard it at all, […]", as well as the formulation "*It seemed that* all the churches boomed for joy". Later, I will discuss whether one should not attribute at least some of such phenomena to the imitation of a child's perspective, rather than to an actual incapability of remembering.

It is when we read: "*I* sometimes hear [the distant speaking of voices]" that the narrator manifests himself explicitly for the first time. So, as I already said, we have to do it with an overt narrator who is not an anonymous, apparently neutral voice. But it is still difficult to determine whether we have to do it with an internal or a zero-focalization. Also this question is going to be discussed in my term paper.

In the following, two assumptions are taken as a basis: the author decided to not restrict the narrator's status either only to the adult, or only to the child. These two points of view do not represent two mutually exclusive options not overlapping at any time. I think that there exists a gray area, with 'adult' and 'child' as the poles at the extremities of an axis (and, respectively, with the several focalization options alternating and merging into each other). Moreover, there are moments in the story where one can argue that certain statements have to be next to the one or the other pole. A close analysis will verify this approach.

I would like to start with the textual signals indicating that it is a matter of an adult who tells his story in flashbacks. Again, I get back to the first paragraph of *A Child's Christmas in Wales,* where the evaluation "was so much like another" can only be made in retrospect by the adult. However, it is 'now' – that is, the narrator not being a child any more – he hears voices from the past. The memories are still very present and influence his life; he can plunge into them and bring out anecdotes of Christmas.

An explicit flashback is "December, *in my memory,* is white as Lapland", and surely one could question whether this is the truth or not, like in the example "Or, if we heard it at all, […]" I have already quoted above, where we clearly have someone who looks back.

The next passage is debatable: we are told that Mrs. Prothero "beat the dinner gong", but is this an omniscient narrator's knowledge, given that the boys were not in the house when she did so? It not clear whether the narrator knew this as a child, or whether he learned it later.

Reading on the short story, we find another instance of an explicit narrator's voice: it says "Years and years ago, when I was a boy", where the adult speaker enumerates what has changed. So far, the narrator seemed to be either omniscient, or at least on the same level as the character in the story, who is himself. However, then the same voice states "But here a small boy says: 'It snowed last year, too. [...]'". The introduction to the direct speech must have been uttered by a different voice, whereas it could be the case that the boy's words are rendered by the first voice, the adult speaker. The narrator does not tell and comment on his own story any more, but the voice switches to the here and now when the telling of this story took place. Elder Olson identified this method, which he calls "pseudo-drama" (42), also in Thomas' poems, and defines it as "the use of dialogue to suggest that the action represented is the interplay among several distinct persons, whereas in fact there is no such interplay because the 'persons' of the dialogue are not distinct" (ibid). For the question of perspective, this means that several voices and points of view, that is, narration and focalization possibilities, are adopted in this passage.

During the dialogue between the speaker and the boy, the adult's and the child's text are given in direct speech, signaled by quotation marks. This is a way a narrator takes a back seat, and tries to remain neutral. Of course he is still there as narrating instance, as Genette says, but he does not relate to a physical manifestation. As far as focalization is concerned, he sees the action from an external position.

Finally, we find one more example for an explicit flashback, also called 'ulterior narration after the events' in Genette ("*I remember that* we went singing"), and another ambiguous statement which we have to locate between internal- and zero-focalization: "we stumbled up the darkness of the drive that night, *each one of us afraid*, [...] and *all of us too brave* to say a word". This could reflect the point of view of an omniscient narrator who can tell about all the character's feelings, or the perspective of the adult who looks back, analyzes, and draws conclusions.

For one thing, I have shown that the adult narrator appears sometimes more, sometimes less explicit, but is never absent. The manifestations one encounters take the form of a conspicuously achronological composition of the story announced by certain phrases, remarks which were made *a posteriori*, and the direct speech of the adult narrator. For another, I distinguished one more manner to identify the latter as such, namely by his ironic comments and comparisons.

We find the first example for such a comment in the third paragraph of the short story. The children play outside and imagine to be "trappers from Hudson Bay, *off Mumbles Road*". The first part describes what the children believed they were, and adopts thus their point of view (see the analysis of the child speaker), whereas the second is an additional comment by the adult narrator on their game.

The same is true for the sentence "in the muffling silence of the eternal snows – *eternal, ever since Wednesday* – [...]", where the comment relativizes the proposition of the preceding part of the sentence. More examples are "Mrs, Prothero was announcing ruin *like a town crier in Pompeii*", "Mr. Prothero standing in the middle of [the clouds and the smoke], waving his slipper *as though he were conducting*", "Easy Hobby-Games for Little Engineers, complete with instructions. *Oh, easy for Leonardo!*", "[the aunts] sat on the very edge of their chairs, poised and brittle, *afraid to break, like faded cups and saucers*", and many more. The perspective changes rapidly, insinuating the ease with with the grandfather switches between present and past.

My following analysis will deal with the textual signals which can be interpreted as seen from a child's perspective. This stylistic choice made by Dylan Thomas is, inter alia, the reason for the work's success. In children's eyes, Christmas is all the more special; they wait for the presents impatiently, everything shines brighter, and being overwhelmed by the magic atmosphere and all the other events, this may lead to exaggerations in a report made by a child. But when they are skilfully employed, as it is definitely the case in *A Child's Christmas in Wales*, the scenes from the past begin to relive. As Sacheverell Sitwell explains: "It is only through truth transcendentalised that the average or approximate can come out. Such are the purposes of exaggeration; for these are in effect the fine plumes of poetry. They make a clearer lens, and magnify the detail" (qtd. by E. Glyn Lewis in Tedlock 171).

In the short story, we find exaggerations like "deadly snowballs", "nobody could have a noisier Christmas", or "mittens made for giant sloths". They not only make us laugh, but also try to point out that childhood memories are subjective. Sometimes, exaggerations occur within a description of the games the children play. The narrator adopts a child's point of view when it comes to the latter's imagination. Cats become jaguars for the narrator and his friend Jim, they behave as if they were "lynx-eyed hunters, [...], fur-capped and moccasined trappers from Hudson Bay", or "Eskimo-footed arctic marksmen". What is more, the surroundings are able to adapt to the children's imaginativeness; and so a normal cat becomes "the neighbor's polar cat", and the Prothero's house, an "igloo".

The way in which the narrator talks about the firemen is characteristic of a child's perception, too. By referring to them as "three tall men in helmets", and then again as "three tall firemen in their shining helmets" which is almost a synecdoche, this could be an attempt of imitating how children look at them, and to show what they see and what is important to them. One can understand that the boys must be fascinated and impressed by the men's uniforms.

The child's voice can also manifest itself in a comment, like "never a catapult", when the useless presents are cited. The speaker apparently regrets this, from which I infer that the narrator is a character-focalizer who has insight in the child's emotions and wishes. One has to be careful here, as comments do not necessarily imply and adult's voice and point of view.

During the conversation between the adult and the child, there is a misunderstanding. In order to draw attention to the boy's way of perceiving – in this case, listening to the story, ask questions and add personal remarks – this is a possibility to imitate the former: "'They [the postmen] knocked on the doors with blue knuckles...' – 'Ours has got a black knocker...'". Due to the phonetic similarity of 'knuckles' and 'knocker', and the paradigmatic relation in which these words stand, it happens to the child to mistake the one for the other.

Another interesting passage is the note on the uncles. The boy would like to know whether they also came for a visit when the narrator still was a child himself: "'Were there Uncles in our house?' – 'There are always Uncles at Christmas. The same Uncles.'". The adult says this as if it was a rule and a matter of fact, insinuating that it cannot be different. This mirrors not only the boy's, but every child's way of thinking. There are things which never change, and as a consequence, they are neither questioned nor perceived as bizarre. When it is Christmas, all uncles and aunts have to be there; and this is true for all children.

When the child goes out to play with his friends in the street, the boys are given their own voice. Their conversation is reported to the reader in direct speech, with the narrating instance intervening rarely. They talk about three subjects: hippos, Mr. Daniel, and the fishes in the sea. Although they are certainly not universal, they are significant for children's behavior. The first part of their conversation shows that they have a lot of fantasy, and that they enjoy creating 'what-if'-scenarios', may they be verisimilar or not ("What would you do if you saw a hippo coming down our street?").

The second part tells us how they plan to mock Mr. Daniel – to play tricks on others is what many many children do, and their capriccios allow the readers to recognize themselves. Also by this means, the short story attains a universal level.

Furthermore, the last part demonstrates that children, as they discover the world, ask numerous questions. Some of them appear hilarious to us, and maybe an adult would never care about the fishes and whether they can see the snow. The boys, however, do not think that they behave in a ridiculous way.

This paragraph in direct speech varies from a zero- to an external focalization. When the narrating instance on the intratextual level is covert and lets the children speak for themselves, the distance separating them from the reader, located on the extratextual level, decreases. This is the reason for the impression to be emotionally touched by Dylan Thomas' work.

One more possibility to imitate a child narrator's point of view I will analyze is the syntactic structure. When we have a look at the connection of sentences and sentence components, the rhetorical figure of the polysyndeton – the "succession of words or phrases linked by conjoining words" (Nünning 67) – immediately catches the eye. For example, the narrator tells us: "*And* we ran down the garden, with the snowballs in our arms, toward the house; *and* smoke, indeed, was pouring out of the dining-room, *and* the gong was bombilating, *and* Mrs. Prothero was announcing ruin like a town crier in Pompeii". The conjunction is employed four times, connecting four independent sentences; and if it had been omitted, the whole passage still would have been grammatical and perfectly comprehensible. Despite that, the events are narrated this way, so as to show an excited child's way of recounting the fire at the Protheros' house. Besides this example, comprising by definition a repetitious aspect, the direct speech of the children exhibits this feature as well:

> "I bet people will think there's been hippos."
> "*What would you do if* you saw a hippo coming down our street?"
> "I'd go like this, *bang!* I'd throw him over the railings *and* roll him down the hill *and* then I'd tickle him under the ear *and* he'd wag his tail."
> "*What would you do if* you saw two hippos?"

> "*Let's* post Mr. Daniel a snow-ball through his letter box."
> "*Let's* write things in the snow."
> "*Let's* write, 'Mr. Daniel looks like a spaniel' all over his lawn."

Moreover, we find:

> *And* a whistle to make the dogs bark to wake up the old man next door to make him beat on the wall with his stick to shake our picture off the wall. *And* a packet of cigarettes: you put one in your mouth *and* you stood at the corner of the street *and* you waited for hours, in vain, for an old lady to scold you for smoking a cigarette, *and then* with a smirk you ate it. *And then* it was breakfast under the balloons.

The excerpt quoted above both shows that the child is so excited by all the presents – hence the fast, almost breathless listing of them – and reveals, on a small scale, the last important way I take into consideration in which the child narrator's perception is stressed, namely the juxtaposition of scenes.

There is no transition from the act of eating the cigarette, and having breakfast. The scenes take place at two different locations, the first outside, the second in the house; yet a passage connecting these scenes is missing. Almost the whole work is made up of successive sequences which do not necessarily have to be in a chronological order: descriptions of the aunts' and uncles' actions, description of the presents, the games with friends, and so forth. The passages are interchangeable, because they are cherished anecdotes which do not depend on a certain context. This composition of the prose poem refers to how children perceive and talk about their experiences of Christmas.

5. *A Child's Christmas in Wales:* The film

The adaptation for television of Dylan Thomas' work has been realized in 1987, directed by Don McBrearty, and adapted by Jon Glascoe and Peter Kreutzer. The main actors are Denholm Elliott, who plays the grandfather, Geraint, and Mathonwy Reeves, in the role of Thomas.

Even though the child in the text version has no name, the decision to call the boy like the author of *A Child's Christmas in Wales* alludes to the assumption that the latter has included autobiographical aspects. This is a very complex stroke of genius as respects the question of perception. One can imagine that either the grandfather embodies Thomas as the real author, which would entail that the adult as narrator not only looks back to the past, but actually sees himself as a child when he looks at his grandson, who feels the same as he did then. Or the author is supposed to be embodied by the boy Thomas, and this, in turn, means that the whole film as story concentrates on the child's perspective who relives Christmases many years ago together with his grandfather. The communication situation in a film resembles the one for theater performances: the events and actions of the characters located on the intradiegetic level are not mediated by a narrator any more. This lack, also called 'absoluteness', is one of the most important features of dramatic texts and theater. The addresser (the entire film cast) and the addressee (the spectators) are collective.

6. Different 'translations' from text to film

In the following, I would like to engage in an analysis of text passages, told in a certain perspectival position and performing the task of illustrating an aspect, which are shown or reported differently in the film. In addition, we encounter scenes that do not exist in the text version at all, but they refer to emotions or points of view which are.

Already at the beginning of the text version, the importance for children of snow at Christmas is stressed. The snow, which has always covered the narrator's hometown in winter, also triggers the latter's memories ("I plunge my hands into the snow and bring out whatever I can find"; "It was snowing. It was always snowing at Christmas. December, in my memory, is white as Lapland"). In the film, this perspective is readopted from the opposite side, so to speak. Like all children, Thomas wants it to snow at Christmas Eve because it simply has to be that way, and we are shown his regret that all he gets is rain. The focus here is on a child's wishes and expectations.

Naturally, the unwrapping of the Christmas presents is among the most important events, too. The text also devotes several paragraphs to the description of the useful and useless presents, but instead of only presenting them, the film includes a sequence in which is discussed the question of what is a 'good' present. According to the parents, socks are useful; however, in the boy's opinion, 'useful' is not equal to 'good', in the meaning of 'suitable for a Christmas present'. The snow dome Thomas receives may not be useful in a strict sense, but is is a beautiful, and, most notably, a personal present from his grandfather. I will consider its role as catalyst in the following chapter.

Another sequence that has been added in the film version is the one in which the child wants to stay awake until Father Christmas comes. This scene's function is it to underline the boy's naiveté on the one hand, but also his curiosity on the other. This unsophisticatedness is not seen contemptuously, quite the contrary: the grandfather remembers how he himself prepared biscuits and a glass of milk, and tried not to fall asleep, of course without success. He recalls how happy he was when he found his presents, and is thus able to put himself in the position of his grandson. At this point in the film, the lines between past and present, between the grandfather's and the boy's feelings, and eventually, between two different positions of perceptions, begin to blur. Thomas' emotions at the here and now in the film are similar to those of his grandfather when he was a child, and together they relive the bygone Christmases, as well as the actual Christmas.

The next scene to be analyzed aims at illustrating the same point as the one above. In the text, the narrator cites as useless present "troops of bright tin soldiers who, if they could not fight, could always run". The child in the text qualifies them as rather boring, whereas in the film, the soldiers do fight because the power of the child's imagination permits them to come to life. We can hear cries, explosions, marching soldiers, the neighing of a horse, and can even see the dust of the canons. The spectators of the film find themselves in the child's position, being able to perceive everything the latter perceives.

Three short sequences, also not present in the text, are a creative addition which points out perceive and evaluate each other, but which does this in a comical way. We see how the young Geraint imitates the waddling of the chapel-goers, their shoulders lifted up, fighting against the wind and the snow. He also imitates a grumpy, elderly man who has scolded him for making a snow angel at the cemetery, as well as two young men who the boy seems to admire. Clearly, these scenes are responsible for setting the atmosphere, arousing sympathy for the boy and for making the spectators smile, but not exclusively. At a more general level, they direct our attention to the question of the point of view. Some adult rules, opinions, and behavior may seem strange, incomprehensible, or as in this case, ridiculous to a child; and of course vice versa.

The next scene I am going to have a look at is the family having dinner. By the technique of fast motion, or 'time lapse', the time seems so move faster, and all actions are accelerated. The more the end of the dinner, crowned by the pudding, approaches, the faster does the music play and the family members eat, drink, and talk. When speeding up the events, the conversations of the characters become unintelligible. This captures the child's perception, who is overwhelmed by all the impressions, the noises, and the delicious meal, so that it cannot really grasp all the input assailing it. Furthermore, this restates what I have analyzed at the beginning of the chapter on the first passages of the text version: being only a child with a limited perspective, and given that the events are recalled many years later, this strengthens the theory of an unreliable, subjective narrator whose accounts are probably not exact.

The last additional sequences I would like to highlight are those dealing with the comparison of Christmas back then, and Christmas nowadays. Whereas the reader of the text version had to be much more attentive in order to detect who was speaking and seeing at a given moment, this is easier for the spectator of the film, who actually sees the narrating grandfather, or the camera position, to which I will come in the passage after next. The first instance is about the look at past and present Christmases from the point of view of the child: when we believe the uncles, what they have in the here and now of the film is nothing compared with Christmas when they were children. This is a play on the phrase children often hear from older family members: 'When I was a child, everything was different, and better!'. But is this true? A little later in the film, we see old Geraint and little Thomas sitting on the sofa, discussing exactly this question. In the boy's opinion, everything that his grandfather has told him so far "sounds like an ordinary Christmas to [him]"; and surprisingly, this is also what Geraint thinks. Instead of claiming that the Christmases of his childhood were special, he seems to hint at that the question whether they were better in the past, or are better in the present, is actually of no importance. As everybody can be young only once, the boy should focus on Christmas now. Also this is something that never changes throughout the time.

The following analysis will deal with the effects of leaps in time and the position of the camera on perspective.

Analogous to the text version of *A Child's Christmas in Wales*, the film sequences alternate between two moments in time, namely the childhood of the grandfather as well as the childhood of Thomas, which bear resemblances to each other and are thus sometimes difficult to distinguish. But just like there were nevertheless identifiable several textual signs or stylistic devices which corroborated my hypothesis of perspectival changes, also the film has its proper possibilities to deal with narration and focalization, camera techniques being one of them.

The first scene takes place in the living-room; Thomas' mother and grandfather are decorating the Christmas tree while the boy is sad because it's raining outside. Very often, the camera is either close to the boy's face in order to focus on his feelings, or at least at the same level as him, following his movements. This choice makes clear that it is a child's point of view that is going to be crucial in the film. Until the first flashback begins, the camera assumes two main positions: about two meters away from Thomas standing in front of the sofa where his parents and his grandfather sit, and next to Thomas, as if the events were seen by him. In addition, when looking at the fire scene more closely, one can also see that the camera is always about as high as the children, and not looking on them from above.

The camera's position is able to show the spectators whether they are watching a scene which takes place in the past, or in the present. We get aware of this when the rain patters against the window of the family's house, indicating that we are back from a flashback in the here and now of the film.

Via camera positions, one can also try to draw the spectators into the story, making them believe to be a part of the action. They feel connected to the characters of the film, which can increase their empathy for them. Furthermore, this is a powerful way to influence opinions and emotions. This is what happens in the scene in which grandfather and grandson are shown, right after the flashback of the fire at the Prothero's. The camera, by maintaining the same distance, moves in a circle around the grandfather who, in turn, directs his speech to the camera, thus to his audience. The spectators are in the same role as Thomas: all are listening carefully, re-experiencing Christmas many decades ago. However, they can also be no neutral, exterior observers, as the scene after the second, very short flashback, shows. The camera switches between close-ups of old Geraint's and Thomas' face. In the first case, the spectator has the same point of view as the boy; in the second, the same as the grandfather. Combining this with the knowledge that past and present sometimes melt into each other, one sees that even in the spectator's situation is mirrored the multiple perspectival possibilities.

Furthermore, via camera movement the plunging into memories can be made explicit. A trigger for reliving Christmas and the nostalgia of the past are the photos Geraint and Thomas are contemplating together. The camera zooms on the photo of Geraint as a boy which comes to live, and we are brought into the past. Likewise, from the flashback via the photo, we get back to the here and now of the film.

The two following sequences I would like to point out are about the children. When we see young Geraint peering into a house where he observes some men ("uncles, most certainly") smoking and coughing. Exactly like the child, the camera is positioned outside and "looks" at the scenes from the same angle of vision. Again, the focalization situation seems to be neutral, but the comments on the men's behavior indicate that everything is perceived through the eyes of a child. The other sequence takes place at the shore: the camera moves with them and accompanies their walk; however, it maintains a constant distance of about five or six meters. When taking the music in the film into account, I will come back to this scene in order to propose an explanation for this choice of position.

Ultimately, I am going to look at the very last flashback of the film. Thomas is already in bed, waiting for his grandfather to tell him a story. While speaking with a candle in his hand, the latter goes slowly around his grandson's bed, and the camera follows him while being fixed approximately where the boy's bed is standing. This position suggests the point of view of the child to whom the camera switches right after, and who we see following his grandfather with his eyes, also turning slightly his head. So, a spectator comes to believe himself to be Thomas, and, generally spoken, in the role of a child at Christmas Eve. This is definitely a reason why Dylan Thomas' work, both the text and the film version, has been acclaimed for reaching out to everybody, touching our hearts. Not only spectator and character are merging, but also character and character, thus, two different perspectives. At the very end, when the grandfather finishes his report with the words "and then I slept", the camera shows his grandson Thomas sleeping, too. The confounding of past and present, as well as the universality of the story, are underlined once more.

My final point of analysis is the role of music; an element the text version, if it is not broadcast in a studio equipped with the necessary techniques, cannot include.

Even before one is able to discern what the characters are doing in the living-room, the

Christmas song with which the film starts already points at the actions (namely the decorating of the tree), locates the story in time, and sets the atmosphere. But these are not the only functions: understanding 'music' in a broad sense, also including shorter sequences of melodies or all sounds produced by instruments, the scene in which Thomas gets a snow dome is important to look at. At the moment in which the boy recognizes what his present is, we hear a music which sounds like little jingling bells, making the present appear all the more special, almost magic. A similar sound rings out at the moment in which we see how the hands of the boys are forming snowballs – this stands of course for the plunging into childhood memories, as the off-speaker has said – , and in general almost always when a flashback begins.

The music also adapts to the character's emotions and actions. When the boys run from the Protheros' house in order to call the fire brigade, the rhythm of the music is fast and accompanies their sprint down the hill. Furthermore, the music is rather joyful than grave, almost like a tarantella, and repeats a short sequence of tones a number of times.

Music can function as an implicit characterization, which one sees in the scene of the snow angel. When an old man catches the boy in the act, not only the first's cantankerous expression indicates his feelings, but also the organ music. It is already played even before the man appears, and could be a means of foreshadowing.

Naturally, music supports the actions and atmosphere of scenes. I have already mentioned the technique of fast motion, used for the family dinner, and of course the music speeds up in accordance with the celerity of the movements. During the children's walk at the sea shore, the music is important just as well. It is much calmer than in other scenes and a choir sings in the backdrop to underline the nostalgia this memory is remembered with. This brings me back to what I have explained concerning the camera position: given that this sequence is laden with the yearning for the past which can only be relived in thoughts, the camera being the eye of the grandfather is unable to be amongst the boys. The distance it retains, emphasized by the music, alludes to the distance with which this scene is recalled.

Finally, music can create a 'bridge' between past and present. The fist scene of the film, taking place at present time, begins with a Christmas song, and the last scene of the flashback is all about music and songs, too. But what is more, the music we hear during the flashback continues to play when we slowly come back to the here and now. It can go on because it is a carrier of memories for everyone and, in many families, it is also an important part of Christmas. Dylan Thomas' work captures the very essence of it – his poetry can be of any age and any place.

7. Conclusion

My term paper first analyzed the text version of Dylan Thomas' *A Child's Christmas in Wales*, which is a composition of two works, a radio talk and an essay. I alluded to the diverging opinions on the author's poems, to which this work also belongs, as well as to the alleged incompatibility of Thomas' and, in this case, the touching report of childhood memories. I introduced Gérard Genette's basic assumptions in narratology: the questions "who sees?" (focalization) and "who speaks?" (narration) have not the same answers. Furthermore, according to him, absolute neutrality in a narrative is an idealization. Genette did not explicitly say that these terms could also be applied to film analyses; nevertheless, I believe especially the aspect of focalization to be enriching in terms of perspective, or effects on the spectators.

Next, I furnished evidence for the affinities with a poem by reverting to the main characteristics as proposed by Nünning. In order to to illustrate these, I dwelled upon the musicality of the work which becomes more evident when it is read out aloud. Here I gave several examples for stylistic features on all linguistic levels. These contribute to the sens of nostalgia and make clear how precious these memories are to the grandfather. The flashbacks are like presents he can open and not only relive, but revive again. Not only the idyllic portrait of Christmas, but also the combination with music, snow, and gifts are what make the story universal. The introductory passages made me reflect upon the narrator's reliability because they – and also other instances – showed that certain details from the past got lost, but not the feelings, or all the sensory and visual impressions. But this is another way of letting us know how the world appears through the eyes of a child. In the following, I concentrated on signs in the text which hint at the point of view of either nearer to an adult or a child perspective. The lines blur, as the possibilities of telling and showing a scene must be seen as being on a scale.

After this, the film version of the work from 1987 has been taken into account. I began with the examination of scenes which have been told differently in the text version – or which in the latter did not exist at all – with respect to the question of perspective. We saw that often the added sequences got back to an idea that was already present in the text, that was showing the events from a child's point of view. For example, little Thomas' joy in Christmas is heightened by suspense. Thus, we are shown the unwrapping of the presents at the beginning. This is the reason why we can say that those scenes are multiple ways a 'translation' of the idea can be done. Moreover, one could recognize that the film relied on 'catalysts' who cause the flashbacks and help the spectators to be informed about the time at which the actions take place. Finally, I turned to the signification of camera techniques and music in the film.

8. Bibliography

A Child's Christmas in Wales. Directed by Don McBrearty. Atlantis Films : 1987. Online
source. <<https://www.youtube.com/watch?v=GrLDaAG7j_o>> (03.11.2013)

Ferris, Paul. *Dylan Thomas.* New York : The Dial Press, 1977.

Fitzgibbon, Constantine. *The Life of Dylan Thomas.* London : J.M. Dent & Sons LTD, 1965.

Genette, Gérard. *Narrative Discourse. An Essay in Method.* Ithaca, New York : Cornell
University Press, 1983.

Goodreads. "Quotable Quote". Online source. <<https://www.goodreads.com/quotes/118916-
christmas---that-magic-blanket-that-wraps-itself-about-us>> (03.11.2013)

Guillemette, Lucie, and Cynthia Lévesque. "Narratology". *Signosemio.* Online source :
<<http://www.signosemio.com/genette/narratology.asp>> (28.10.2013)

Korg, Jacob. "Dylan Thomas's Concept of the Poet". In *Dylan Thomas: Craft or Sullen Art.* Ed.
Alan Bold. London : Vision Press, 1990. (15-34)

Lewis, E. Glyn. "Dylan Thomas". In *Dylan Thomas: The Legend and the Poet. A Collection of
Biographical and Critical Essays.* Ed. E.W. Tedlock. Westport : Greenwood Press,
²1975. (168-175)

Nünning, Vera and Ansgar. *An Introduction to the Study of English and American Literature.*
Stuttgart : Klett Verlag, 2009.

Olson, Elder. *The Poetry of Dylan Thomas.* Chicago and London : The University of Chicago
Press, 1954.

Patron, Sylvie. "On the Epistemology of Narrative Theory : Narratology and Other Theories of
Fictional Narrative". In *The Travelling Concept of Narrative.* Eds. Hyvärinen, Matti,
Anu Korhonen and Juri Mykkänen. Helsinki : Helsinki College for Advanced Studies,
2006. (118-133)

Stearns, Marshall W. "Unsex the Skeleton : Notes on the Poetry of Dylan Thomas". In *Dylan
Thomas: The Legend and the Poet. A Collection of Biographical and Critical Essays.*
Ed. E.W. Tedlock. Westport : Greenwood Press, ²1975.

The Sunday Guardian. "Christmas Traditions & Dylan Thomas's read-aloud verses". Online
source : <<http://www.sunday-guardian.com/bookbeat/christmas-traditions-a-dylan-
thomass-read-aloud-verses>> (31.10.2013)

Thomas, Dylan. "A Child's Christmas in Wales". In *Dylan Thomas – poems.* Ed.
poemhunter.com. 2012. p. 9-13. Online source <<http://www.poemhunter.com/i/
ebooks/pdf/dylan_thomas_2012_3.pdf>> (28.10. 2013)